A N
Butterfly

My First Look at Metamorphosis

Written by Pamela Hickman
Illustrated by Heather Collins

Kids Can Press

This is the tree

that Connie climbs.

A tree is home to many hidden creatures.

Can you find these creatures under the bark?

carpenter ant

sow bug

tree borer

tree borer grub

bark beetle

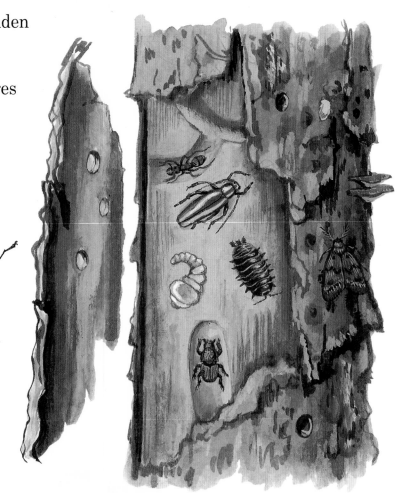

This is the leaf

that grows on the tree

that Connie climbs.

A leaf has veins, just like you.

The lines you see carry food and water inside the leaf.

This is the butterfly
that landed on the leaf,
that grows on the tree
that Connie climbs.

All butterflies have four wings.

The wings are covered with tiny scales that give them their patterns and colors.

cabbage

monarch

red admiral

comma

swallowtail

mustard white

This is the egg
that was laid by the butterfly,
that landed on the leaf,
that grows on the tree
that Connie climbs.

Peek inside the butterfly's egg.

When the tiny caterpillar is ready,
it chews a hole to get out.

This is the caterpillar
that hatched from the egg,
that was laid by the butterfly,
that landed on the leaf,
that grows on the tree
that Connie climbs.

A caterpillar eats so much that it outgrows and sheds its skin many times.

This is called molting.

Before it molts, a new, larger skin forms under the old one.

1 week

2 weeks

3 weeks

This is the chrysalis
that was made by the caterpillar,
that hatched from the egg,
that was laid by the butterfly,
that landed on the leaf,
that grows on the tree
that Connie climbs.

A caterpillar's body changes completely while it is inside the chrysalis.

During this time it does not eat or move around.

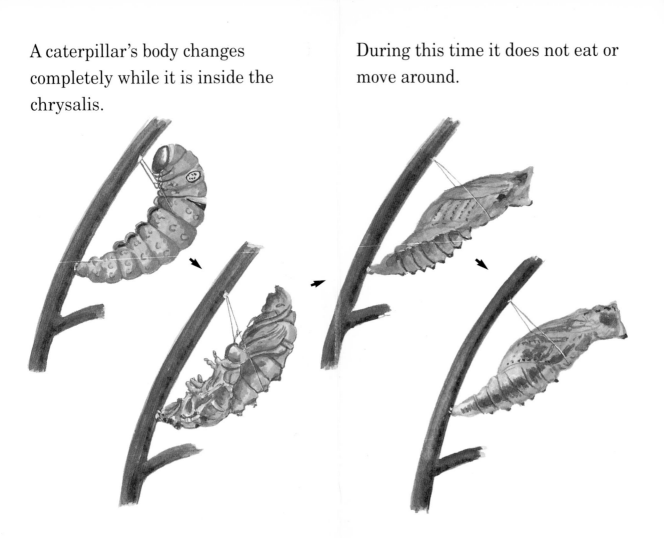

This is the new butterfly
that came out of the chrysalis,
that was made by the caterpillar,
that hatched from the egg,
that was laid by the butterfly,
that landed on the leaf,
that grows on the tree
that Connie climbs.

A butterfly drinks flower nectar with its tubelike mouth.

When the butterfly is finished, its mouth coils up like a party blower.

How beautiful!